I0633169

tewart, Melissa.
ow do fish breathe
nderwater? /
2007.
3305218307647
1   01/13/10

HOW DO FISH BREATHE UNDERWATER?

MELISSA STEWART

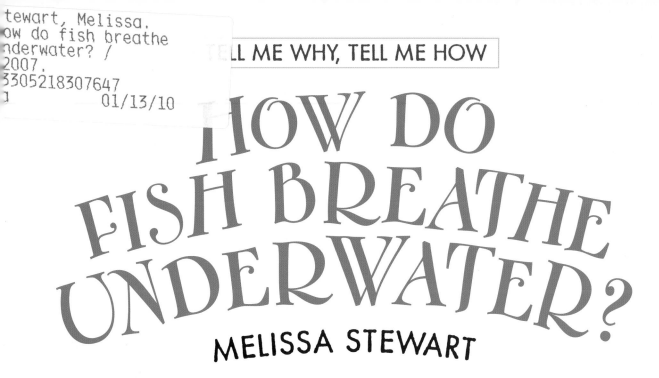

 **Marshall Cavendish**
Benchmark
New York

Marshall Cavendish
99 White Plains Road
Tarrytown, New York 10591-9001
www.marshallcavendish.us

Copyright © 2007 by Marshall Cavendish Corporation
First Marshall Cavendish paperback edition, 2008

All rights reserved. No part of this book may be reproduced or utilized in any form or by any means electronic or
mechanical, including photocopying, recording, or by any information storage and retrieval system, without
permission from the copyright holders.

All Web sites were available and accurate when this book was sent to press.

Editor: D. Sanders
Editorial Director: Michelle Bisson
Art Director: Anahid Hamparian
Series Designer: Alex Ferrari

Library of Congress Cataloging-in-Publication Data

Stewart, Melissa.
How do fish breathe underwater? / by Melissa Stewart.
p. cm. — (Tell me why, tell me how)
Summary: "An examination of the phenomena of scientific principles behind
the ability of fish to extract oxygen from water"—Provided by publisher.
Includes bibliographical references.

ISBN 978-0-7614-3365-1 (PB)
ISBN 978-0-7614-2109-2 (HB)

1. Fishes—Respiration. I. Title. II. Series.

QL639.1.S73 2006
573.2'17—dc22

2005017258

Photo research by Candlepants Incorporated

Cover photo: Werner H. Muller/Peter Arnold Inc.

The photographs in this book are used by permission and through the courtesy of: *Peter Arnold Inc.:* Secret Sea
Visions, 1; Paul Springett, 12. *SuperStock:* age fotostock, 6, 13, 20, 21, 25; SuperStock, Inc, 9. *Corbis:* More/zefa,
5; Randy Faris, 16; Warren Morgan, 18. *Photo Researchers Inc;* Jeff Rotman, 10, 22, 23; Dave Roberts, 19.
Minden Pictures: Norbert Wu, 14, 26. *Bernard Photo Productions/Animals Animals/Earth Scenes:* 24.

Printed in Malaysia
3 5 6 4 2

CONTENTS

Just like people, fish need oxygen to survive.
Unlike people, fish can get oxygen from water.

~ The Breath of Life ~

All day and all night, you breathe without even thinking about it. Have you ever wondered why?

It is because your body needs **oxygen**—one of the gases in air—to survive. Without oxygen, all the different parts of your body could not do their jobs. Your heart could not pump blood. Your stomach could not break down food. Your brain could not think.

Most of the time, you breathe without thinking about it. But you must take in a deep breath before going underwater.

5

These fish get all the oxygen they need from the water they live in.

Why is oxygen so important? It helps your body get **energy** from the foods you eat. Energy gives your body the power it needs to live and grow.

People are not the only animals that need a constant flow of oxygen. Dogs and dolphins, snakes and snails, frogs and fish all depend on this important gas. Whether an animal lives on land or in the water, it must keep on breathing so its body can work.

Now I Know!
Animals need what important gas to survive?

Oxygen.

Nutrients from the foods we eat mix with oxygen to give us the energy we need every day.

Getting Oxygen

Each time you inhale, fresh air enters your nose and mouth. The air rushes over your voice box, travels down your windpipe, and moves into your lungs.

Once there, the oxygen from the air moves into your blood. Then your heart pumps the blood to all the **cells** in your body.

When oxygen enters your cells, it mixes with **nutrients.** These nutrients come from the foods you eat. When oxygen and nutrients combine, they give off energy. Your body needs that energy to live and grow.

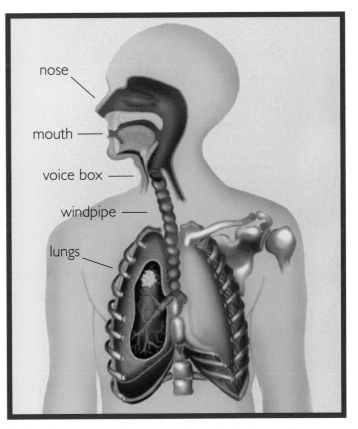

nose

mouth —

voice box —

windpipe —

lungs

In the human respiratory system, air is drawn in through the nose and mouth.

9

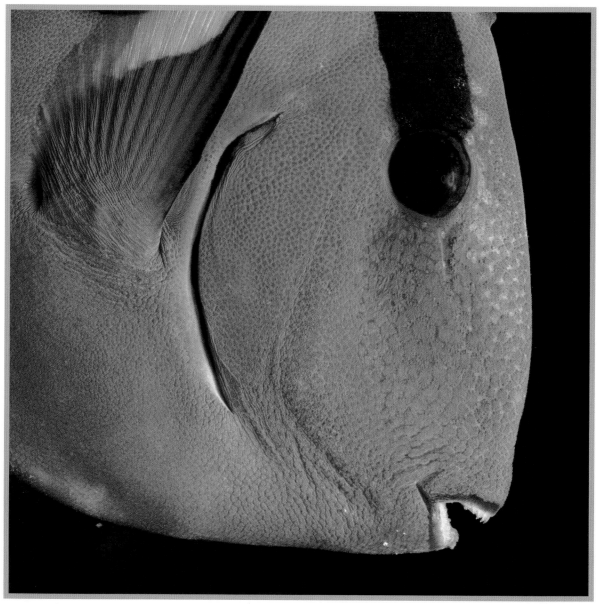

Like all fish, this Indo-Pacific bluetang does not have lungs. It has a different kind of respiratory system.

As your body uses oxygen, it makes another gas called **carbon dioxide.** You do not need carbon dioxide to live. So every time you **exhale,** or breathe out, your lungs push carbon dioxide out of your body.

It is similar for fish. Only fish do not have lungs, and they do not breathe air. So they must get all the oxygen they need from the water that surrounds them their entire lives.

Now I Know!

Every time you breathe out, what gas do you exhale?

Carbon dioxide.

Compare this fish to the fossil
shown on the next page.
Modern fish look similar to fish
that lived long ago.

Living Underwater

About 500 million years ago, a new group of animals appeared in Earth's oceans. These creatures, called **vertebrates,** were unlike any other animals. Each one had a backbone and a skeleton inside its body. The oldest known vertebrate **fossil** was of a small fishlike creature. It had no jaws or teeth. Its body was covered with thick, bony plates.

The fossil shows a fish that lived about 50 million years ago.

Strong, sharp teeth, like the ones on this harlequin tuskfish, help fish survive.

As time passed, fish developed jaws with strong, sharp teeth. Scales formed in place of bony plates. Because scales are strong, they protect a fish's body like a suit of armor. And because scales are light, they make it easy for a fish to swim through the water.

Today, more than 25,000 **species,** or kinds, of fish can be found in Earth's oceans, lakes, and rivers. Their bodies are perfectly designed to survive in a watery world.

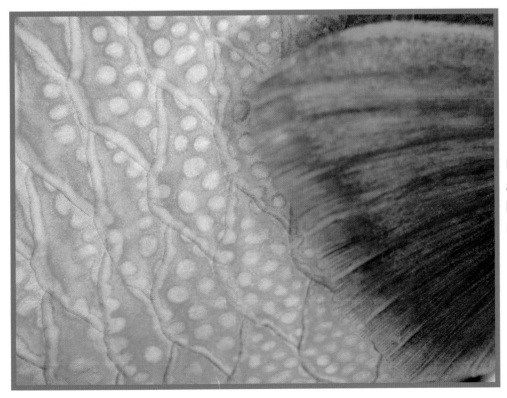

Light and strong, a fish's scales help protect its body.

Like air, water is made up of many different materials. One of those materials is oxygen. But water contains less oxygen than air does. So a fish's body has to work hard to get the oxygen it needs. A person's lungs take in only about 25 percent of the oxygen in the air. But some fish can remove up to 80 percent of the oxygen in water.

Fish must make good use of the oxygen they take in. They must waste as little energy as possible.

Fins help fish stop, start, turn, or cruise through the water.

The shape of their bodies helps. It allows them to glide gracefully through the water. Thin, light fins make it easy for a fish to start, stop, and turn. People use a lot of energy to move their arms and to kick their legs when they swim. But fish are experts at moving through the water.

Now I Know!

What part of a fish's body helps it to stop, start, and turn in the water?

Fins.

A fish uses its swim bladder to change
its depth or position in the water.

Designed for the Deep

A fish's body is specially designed to not waste energy. It is also perfectly made for moving through water as easily as people can move on the land. Many fish have a **swim bladder**. This unique body part helps fish float. It also allows them to rise to the surface or sink to the bottom. As a result, they don't have to use energy to swim up or down. When a fish wants to move toward the surface, it pumps air into its swim bladder. The fish's body becomes lighter and begins to rise. When the fish wants to return to deeper water, it lets air out of its swim

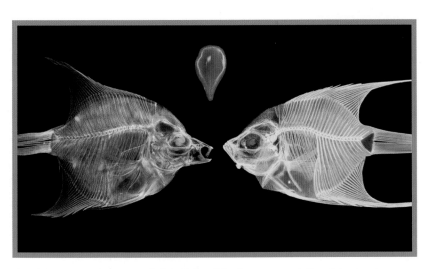

As this x-ray shows, a fish's light thin bones and flexible body are perfectly designed for life in the water.

bladder. The fish's body becomes heavier and sinks toward the bottom. A swim bladder is just one of the special body parts that help many fish survive underwater.

The way a fish looks—the colors and patterns of its scales—also help it to survive. Many land animals run away from their enemies. But running takes a lot of energy. That is why most fish hide from their **predators.** Brightly colored sea horses and clown fish blend in with coral reefs, so enemies can't see them. A flounder's speckled or spotted scales match the sandy seafloor. A catfish's dark, slimy skin makes it hard to spot in slow-moving, murky water.

Bass, pike, and other fish that live in open waters have dark backs and pale bellies. When the sun shines down

This thorny sea horse lives along Australia's Great Barrier Reef. Its bright colors help it blend in with the coral reef.

20

Fish must avoid predators that live in and out of the water.

through the water, these fish seem to disappear. Their backs match the dark water below them, so birds, bears, and snakes cannot spot them. When otters, sea lions, or bigger fish look up from below, the pale bellies blend with the light from above. Tricks like this help fish stay safe without using too much energy. What keeps a fish's energy flowing is the oxygen it gets from the water it lives in.

Now I Know!

What body part helps a fish float, rise, and sink in the water?

The swim bladder.

Fish do not have lungs. Fish must get the oxygen they need another way. Do you know how?

How Do Fish Breathe Underwater?

Like you, a fish has a **respiratory system.** This group of organs works together to help an animal get the oxygen it needs to survive. The most important part of your respiratory system is your lungs. They help you remove oxygen from the air.

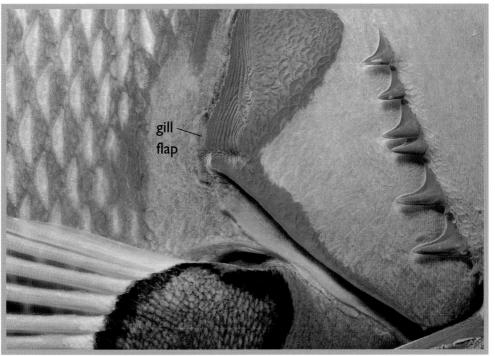

gill flap

The gills of this queen angelfish are protected by a flap of skin.

But fish live in the water. Their bodies are not surrounded by air. Lungs cannot remove oxygen from water, so fish have **gills** instead. They are found just behind a fish's mouth. Gills are the most important part of a fish's respiratory system.

To get oxygen, a fish gulps water and pumps it over the gills. As water moves over the thin walls of the gills, oxygen passes into the fish's blood. Then the fish's tube-shaped heart pumps the blood to all the cells in the fish's body.

Inside the fish's cells, the oxygen mixes with nutrients from food to create energy. Just like you, a fish needs energy to live and grow.

As a fish's body uses up oxygen, it makes carbon dioxide (just like a person's body). The extra carbon dioxide is picked up by water passing through the

A close-up view of a salmon's gills.

As these fish swim, water moves though their bodies. Their gills are constantly working, removing oxygen from that water.

Fish and people may look different, but they all need oxygen to survive.

fish's gills. It is then carried out of the fish's body.

So even though you live on land and fish live in water, a fish's body is not all that different from yours. Fish and people may look different on the outside, but their insides have more in common than you might think.

Now I Know!
What do fish use to take oxygen from the water?

Their gills.

Activity

People cannot remove oxygen from water, and most fish cannot remove oxygen from the air. That means you can swim underwater only until you have used up all the oxygen in your lungs. The next time you go to a lake or a swimming pool, take along a watch with a second hand. Ask an adult to time how long you can hold your breath underwater.

An animal that lives in or near the water can hold its breath much longer than a person can. Take a look at the chart below.

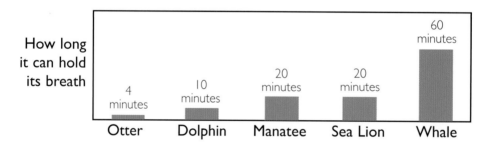

How long it can hold its breath

Otter	Dolphin	Manatee	Sea Lion	Whale
4 minutes	10 minutes	20 minutes	20 minutes	60 minutes

How long were you able to stay underwater? Find out how long friends and family members can hold their breath underwater. Then make a chart like the one above. Include each person's name and his or her time.

 Glossary

carbon dioxide—An invisible gas that animals create when they release energy from food.

cell—The basic building block of all living things.

energy—Something that provides creatures with the power to carry out body processes.

exhale—To breathe out.

fossil—Evidence of a plant or animal that once lived on Earth.

gill—The body organ that allows oxygen to pass from water into a fish's bloodstream. Some other water animals also have gills.

inhale—To breathe in.

nutrient—A tiny bit of food that the body can break down to release energy.

oxygen—An invisible gas that animals need so they can release energy from food.

predator—An animal that kills and eats other animals.

respiratory system—All the organs in an animal's body that help it take in oxygen.

species—A group of similar creatures that can mate and produce healthy young.

swim bladder—A body organ that helps many fish species control their position in the water.

vertebrate—An animal with a backbone. Birds, frogs, snakes, mice, and people are all vertebrates.

Find Out More

BOOKS

Bailey, Jill. *How Fish Swim.* New York: Benchmark Books, 1997.

LeVert, Suzanne. *The Lungs.* New York: Benchmark Books, 2002.

Ricciuti, Edward R. *Fish.* Woodbridge, CT: Blackbirch Press, 1993.

Ruiz, Andres Llamas. *Animals on the Inside.* New York: Sterling, 1994.

Stille, Darlene R. *The Respiratory System.* Danbury, CT: Children's Press, 1997.

WEB SITES

Cool Kids: Fishin'

http://www.ncfisheries.net/kids/

Learn about the role of fish in the food chain and how to identify parts of fish. You can also read some fun "fish tales."

Fish Information Service

http://fins.actwin.com/

Would you like to keep a pet fish? Check out this site before you head to your local pet store. You can also find a list of public aquariums. There's probably one near your home.

Index

Page numbers for illustrations are in **boldface.**